SHIFTING
THE SILENCE

ETEL ADNAN

SHIFTING THE SILENCE

NIGHTBOAT BOOKS
NEW YORK

© 2020 by Etel Adnan
All rights reserved
Printed in the United States
Third Printing, 2022

ISBN: 978-1-64362-030-5

Excerpts of *Shifting the Silence* were published in
frieze and *One Grand Journal*.

Cover art by Etel Adnan, *Untitled*, 1991,
pastel on paper, courtesy of the artist
and Callicoon Fine Arts, New York

Design and typesetting by Rissa Hochberger
Text set in Bodoni

Cataloging-in-publication data is available
from the Library of Congress

Nightboat Books
New York
www.nightboat.org

*Shifting
the Silence*

Yes. The shifting, after the return of the tide, and my own. A question rushes out of the stillness, and then advances an inch at a time: has this day ever been before, or has it risen from the shallows, from a line, a sound?

When we name things simply, with words preceding their meaning, a cosmic narration takes place. Does the discovery of origins remove the dust? The horizon's shimmering slows down all other perceptions. It reminds me of a childhood of emptiness which seems to have taken me near the beginnings of space and time.

Now, dark animals roam in the forest, you could touch them. A particular somnolence takes hold of you when the shadows start growing. Then, the heart creates different beats. You want to touch the leaves, look intensely at each tree. The night falls, already tired, already bare.

1

The size of the future is not any longer than this alley's. And questions are falling, and failing. But to go by a narrow gully, find the tide at its lowest, watch ducklings follow their mother in search of evening food, is a sure way to some kind of an illumination.

I am wearing the rose color of Syria's mountains and I wonder why it makes me restless. Often my body feels close to sea creatures; sticky, slimy, unpredictable, more ephemeral than need be. From there I have to proceed, as an avalanche of snow falls. That's what the radio has just said: that entire villages have been made invisible. But they are faraway: the news never covers my immediate environment.

And having more memories than yearnings, searching in unnameable spaces, Sicily's orchards or Lebanon's thinning waters, I reach a land between borders, unclaimed, and stand there, as if I were alone, but the rhythm is missing.

What is not missing is fear. It's a matter of arteries clogged, of long hours of sleeplessness, of the lack of resolution for any outstanding problem. My feet are sliding on a wet floor, but I have to thank my good luck: I leave the horizon deal with my terror.

Why, oh why!

I miss the cosmic energy of ancient Greece. They loved their gods to whom everything was given save the supreme power. Free, none of them were in the absolute sense, only Zeus was, though his arbitrariness was often looked at with a critical eye. Prometheus was chained because he rebelled, and Io was condemned to suffer an opposite but equally radical punishment, to turn and turn and never rest. There was a raw cruelty to their world, but I miss them, just the same.

To put one's feet on the rocks of Delphi is worth damnation. And to Sikiyonou the offerings for the oracle are still coming. For me, the pain of dying is going to be the impossibility of visiting that site one more time.

When you have no way to go anywhere, what do you do? Of course, nothing. But that's no answer. We let so many replies go unformulated, as a liberation of sorts, so many tides uselessly advance, so many desires are buried (the mind gets tired too). In the middle of the night I measure the cold outside, the silence.

To speak Greek is to use most of Aristotle's own words. But I rely on Eschylus. He reminds me of the mystics from Bukhara. He placed Prometheus on Mount Aetna, linking him to Empedocles. How can one live away from their circle?

But, returning to my condition, if I had to choose a place to spend the night, what would it be? At this point, I will turn my back and go into my room. The major part of the beauty of the world I will ignore, if not all.

4

There are so many islands I dreamed of visiting, where have they gone? They're probably lying where they have always been. Do they possess a consciousness all of their own? I would think so. They are probably like the peacock who recognized me after all the years I had been absent, when he made a loud sound, of a kind I had never heard, and made me joyful. He stirred a kinship between us.

That was at the end of a game for a world championship, a European football game. England against Colombia; the British team playing war, the South Americans playing for the fun of it, always the same story. The peacock followed the excitement, it was late at night and he couldn't sleep.

My thoughts drip, not unlike the faucet. They don't let me know what they're about. Other ones follow, strangers equally.

The daylight is getting dim. We're not in winter, no, we're somewhere in early July. The sunset will happen soon. Then it will disappear too.

Dreams lack any power of decision, but come in bunches, flood the spirit, shake the bones. They favor love-making while we refuse what we yearn for. Watching sunset after sunset doesn't heat the house.

Watching the hours go by doesn't help either. Thus, we're cornered. I leave my door open, pretending it's because of my difficulty breathing, but nothing is true. Better to admit that with the passing of days we know less about just everything. Let's let things roll their own ways, whenever they have some.

I am not used to asking for help, but on what kind of a ground am I standing? An incantation puts me to rest, at last, in undue hours. With eyes swollen we try to see the here, and the overthere, never sure, always dissatisfied. Let's wait even when we don't know what for, a faint line on the horizon always more welcome than this void.

We have lost the liturgies under the wars, the bombings, the fires we went through. Some of us didn't survive, and they were many. The Greeks had their exuberant gods, the sunrise over Mount Olympus. The Canaanites had Mount Sannin. We have our own private mountains, but are they already too tired from waiting for us? I have no roads to them, no wires. In their splendor let them be.

There's a dance of fireflies, little lights turning around the boats of the Bay, tiny creatures chanting, fish jumping—the feast of early summer subsiding in the heat, and lemonades!

We try to subvert the gods, buy their powers, corrupt their souls—we, a race of mercenaries. A tide of mud is moving on the shore, messing the shoreline. Sounds are raining. How many tomorrows do I have to worry about? A cup of tea doesn't taste like ice cream, but it will do. Tea in the evening, unlike the British.

There were times when to be overlooked by death created sacred terror, and those times have returned. The rivers continued to run. I followed some, and others I drew. Most frequently they came as dreams, some were of an amazing magnitude, others mixed their waters in oversized waterfalls. I loved them in all instances. But death, I didn't.

Death abandoned us, not coming when it was due, not answering. Its enemy, a form of life unstoppable, I mean the Oceans, used to appear on stage for events of gigantic dimensions. They spoke human languages besides their own. We pushed them back gradually, polluted them to the brim. We heard not a single cry.

Io cannot die. Prometheus cannot rest. The oceans are helpless. As for us, we can neither live, nor disappear. The stars, at night, emit sparks with the rhythm of our breath. My window is blessed. It opens in daylight on the fields of Greece, that's what I'm trying to believe.

Almost all of my beliefs have deserted me. I take it as a kind of liberation, and anyway, they were never too many. Our houses are cluttered, our minds too, so a fire as devastating as it can be, can well clear the air, enlarge the space, make room for some silence. Year after year all we do is gather dust.

Prometheus rebelled, and Zeus died many centuries later. Large areas of snow replace the banquets which were held by the gods on Mount Olympus. Skiers prefer things as is. I don't know what I would do if I could move more easily around. I would start with Delphi, that's sure. I may desire to die there. The stones of Delphi, in midsummer, are sizzling hot. They burn one's skin, and one's heart. Revelation is abundant over there.

I need to simplify my thinking: to come to the roots of the olive trees I have planted on my island, sit close to them, look at every leaf. Start early in the morning. Then close my eyes and let the morning sun touch my face. Go to the Mediterranean at the street corner, go into its water, its salt, its acid colors, its heat. Oh Lord, let's stop thinking. Let's just be, and for many hours in a row, merge with this vegetal and metallic kind of consciousness which is so overpowering.

And they just told me the saga of this young man from Thessaloniki, so handsome, they said, who was hit by the bullet of a hunter with whom he was on an outing, an accident, they said. Knowing that he was condemned to die, he had hired four guys with a stretcher and paid them to take him to Delphi.

They arrived. The oracle was long gone. He knew it. He thought that the very place would save him. It did, but not the way he expected. It made him experience a sacred geometry, usually reserved to the initiate. But being there was in itself an initiation; he understood that. He watched the sun for the last time.

We have to reconnect what words separated. The hell with Aristotle, though the most misunderstood of all philosophers! I'd rather give back the leaves to the tree, the waves to the sea.

Word-languages are a trap, aren't they? They created chaos and made us sink in incoherence. When someone tells you "I love you," all he means is that he needs some orange juice for his thirst. That explains why so many of us spent a lifetime on poor literature (and once in a while on a masterpiece such as *War and Peace*).

Our words don't suit prophecies anymore. That power is left to other species: to oak trees, for example, to the tides, which through their restlessness carry a phosphorescence we're not equipped to hear.

To sit on a beach and rest our aged bones, that's already a privilege. And to stop the car by a curve and throw an eye on a blazing horizon, that's a victory, but not to sleep at night because of some memories' sheer weight means what?

There are still cathedrals with silent corners in them, dispersed over the world. We have to cover miles. There's also a particular silence to some mountains, vast expanses unfolding and not stirring, standing next to the sound of their waters, in distinct areas, with caves under cliffs. And when deer sleep, you know they ask you to watch over their safety, and most of the time you say yes, you will.

I'm telling you: we're carried by tornadoes we barely notice, whirlwinds we barely feel, aggressions we barely acknowledge, because we're half awake. Things are translated into something alien.

So we searched so much, in erratic ways, didn't find much. We even returned empty-handed. Time is slippery. With our hands made of wheels, as we said long ago, fortune was not on our side, and we didn't ask questions. Then, what did we do?

When stacks of nightmares were delivered to my door, I pretended that I was looking for houses with huge gardens around, but that was a game, a poor game. I was trying, very regularly, to convince myself that I was alive, and that was still another game, and the world fell apart. I had a rendez-vous with some sort of destiny, and I arrived late, very late. The sunset had subsided. Only a few lines, badly lit, were still lingering on the sky. I cried, oh not too much, but I sat and cried.

What did I do next? My memory here is failing, for lack of use, probably, as I tend to "put order" in my past as I do in my drawers. Yes, the house is cluttered, the brain too. We're people of accumulation, and therefore, ironically, of waste. I dream of a room with no furniture, of a past with very few friends, of a country with no weapons. We are tired beyond our capacities for renewal. Oh, what's left!

Dark animals return to the forest, just to be swallowed by huge waves that leave huge masses of wine colored areas on the ocean's darkened surfaces, and I am asking for help, merging my voice to the winds'.

Today is yesterday's tomorrow. That's how it goes. An avalanche of negative ideas is trying to clean itself out to no avail: the old alliance of Greece and Arabia has been broken because we're not looking at the world properly, not creating these strings of words that correspond to what we're seeing. We have lost the whole for its parts;

14

Prometheus gave us fire not for burning every-
thing that's alive, but to light the sky, and now,
even our inner fire is burning out. Are we sane?
I guess we are, and that's the danger, as sanity
wants to keep the fires going.

Fires are proliferating, indeed. One can say that
Hiroshima was a mega-bonfire, a defining one.
The rest of the world slept very well that night.
And we slept last night when Rafina, Athens'
most pristine harbor, burned. There must have
been some of Zeus' descendants among the
dead. The matter is not that they died, but that
we didn't cry.

That takes me back to the love for funerals I had
when I was still too young to start kindergar-
ten. Those funerals were a neighborhood affair.
I would run to the window and see old men,
blind men opening up a procession and chant-
ing prayers, followed by men crying silently, and
some of them carrying the coffin, and a few more

men following, the storekeepers standing by their doors. I was awe-struck.

I was also following the Christian funerals, which were more animated, as women participated. The ones for important people were headed by banners and musicians. I still hear the loud music, a particular music moving between a dirge and a fanfare. So little was happening in those days, but each happening was seen as through a magnifying glass. In fact, every public event seemed to have an epic dimension.

Can we keep that strange sense of sacredness that we knew, as if by inheritance, in our old days? I think we sometimes do, as in this evening, when in a lost corner of Brittany, us the strangers, are united not by hazard but by affinities, even if those are light like air, like clouds passing over our heads. But isn't air the first element that life uses? Barrett's and Carla's travelling to this place is a central event; it will join the experiences and all

16

the stuff that keeps creating what we call eternity...It took a table and few sips of wine to discover the clarity of their profound simplicity.

You know, sunsets are violently beautiful, I would say that they are so by definition, but there are lights, not even colorful in the habitual sense, lights elemental, mercurial, silvery, sulfurous, copper-made, that make us stop, then lose balance, make us open our arms not knowing what else to do, arrest us as if struck by lightning, a soft lightning, a welcome one. I wait for those lights, I know some of you do too, wherever you are, I mean when you are standing by an ocean, alone, within the calmness of your spirit. Be planetary.

I want to go to those places that my dreams open up or that are discovered on postcards or advertisements. This could be pathetic, but it is not, as its intensity redeems it. Tonight I looked on the internet at red mountains in Southern

France. They're made of porphyrus. They're as red as some mountains in Oman, some others in Arizona. We're on a planet sustained by nothing, carried through pure space by a willful star made of fire and in constant ebullition. We're travelers covering traveling grounds. Going, always going.

I threw away my compass to the waves. It had been used by the Arab travelers to China, and, unfortunately, by the colonizers that followed, too. I threw it. I don't know and don't want to know what's coming next, because I also did away with my curiosity.

What's left? This season of heat and wind, this dinner tonight, and these large bands of trembling waves of various shades of green that split my heart with their incredible beauty.

We're witnessing the last days of this civilization as we know it. Through the glass panels of the apartment I observe the ocean. Then something stirs. Things appear, we say, transcending themselves. You call it Being, you call it this wave. It could be people, too.

I didn't sleep last night. Right now the ocean is a flat metallic sheet running from east to west. The reverberation hurts my eyes, but I am happy.

Days go by, but bring surprises. Friends come, and they're messengers, birds of good omen. They lift the sky, and we need it. I do my best to walk by this edge of the town, by the tide. One step at a time. One hour goes by after another. Then the sun launches new rays.

The radio says that Paris is experiencing a heat wave. The temperature will rise to 40° Celsius. This is tropical weather, and nothing assures us that the heat will not go higher. It's even warmer in Brittany. The fish is calling for help. As I am, often, these days.

We lost one more friend from the community of poets. Kevin Killian withdrew from our world. We will miss his powers of affection. Goodbye dear friend. Dear San Francisco, cry for him.

This afternoon, Barrett Watten unveiled his Plan B. He keeps the pulse of the world as it goes its crazy way. He mentioned the "turbulence of destiny." It was sudden, and it worked. Destiny had become a distant notion, a concept, and had thus lost its punch. And then Barrett brings it to life, in my room, of all places. I wonder: Zeus must have died by now, as Aeschylus had pointed to that possibility already when he was dealing with Prometheus. So who's left? The gods have left us, we accepted this emptiness they left behind. (Of course, there's One in whom many believe, He's somewhere—though nowhere—but we do not count Him among the Greeks).

Barrett suggests that destiny is still manifest, and is in turbulence, and is young, for sure, and among us, not an abstraction, but an active element, destiny as his own kind of god. The ever renewed god of the gods is running the Plan. By showing the utter failure of our world, brought about by the failure of Meaning itself, Barrett tries to define what's waiting beyond the boundaries, an urgent explosion (?) foresees the coming, or the necessity of an urgent shift of destiny away from the cycle of the eternal return of the same, beyond whatever already is.

So what do we do, in between, besides eating oysters for dinner, and going for walks, and taking trains or flights…and melting our eyes in the next horizon. This is a way of not giving up.

But the noise rising from the lower floors of the building is not the ocean's roar, and it's tiring my soul. I had lunch in the garden, under a tree, not an oak tree, a tree whose name I forgot. But I didn't forget the freshness of the air in the midst of this heat. A garden! Once in a while, its magic works, like it did today, a breeze circulating in the branches. One of those trees is a magnolia thriving in this non-tropical country. There are also down there weeds, grass, some timid flowers.

The owner of the pancake café sat near me. She spoke of her man with a sweet tone of voice, telling me that he circled the world some three times in his life. Now, he's building a boat, she said, a tiny boat she insisted, just to sail with her in the bay. Our guys are great sailors, she said, and added: great builders! It's true that he recently built a shack for her, a structure hidden by a lot of vegetation around. I thought: such pleasures are getting to be rare.

I'm back to Barrett, to Plan B, to Destiny. It occurs to me that the ocean's destiny is similar to Sisyphus's: the latter pushed the stone up, and let it fall, and pushed it up again, and again…and the ocean comes up, and recedes, and advances again, and nobody, god, angel, human or animal, can do anything to change this state of affairs. The ocean, itself so turbulent, is still bound, like

Prometheus, not to a mountain, but to a pendular merciless movement.

And strangely enough, I'm thinking of Picasso's late drawings and etchings, his erotic pictures where his women are pictured always with their sex conspicuously open, and with men, usually buttoned up, smaller in size, sitting next to them. In a flash, I saw his flagrant kinship to Goya: Goya depicted the horrors of war; Picasso depicts the terror of another war, the one between men and women as he lived it, inevitable, never won, never totally lost, so recurring.

Most people take war in their stride. It's probably wise. Some of them gather metals or other residues of bombs, and make daggers with such debris. Out of weapons which are for mega-killings other weapons are made, rather artistic, and deadly on a private scale. But death is singular, killing one or many is equally unacceptable, and there's no consolation in such matters.

And the killing goes on, and has reached the point where it becomes a matter of personal survival to accept it, and we see morality as a luxury we can do without. The bloody feast goes on, and we stare at it with total hopelessness.

The thing left to do is to be willing to go to the end of just anything, like burning your eyes, metaphorically and physically, by staring long enough at the sun, like when you were a child (in Beirut), and tears were running down. Those were moments transcending.

The conducting line in my soul's deepest layer is reddition, not in the sense of the surrender of a defeated general, but like in the Homeric narration of the Trojan War. It means that I followed lines I never saw, went on unchartered roads, didn't emerge from any confusion. The present was forever blowing.

The Trojan War ended at the Dardanelles. I should have spent my life explaining how I came to that conclusion, but I didn't, and have no regrets. What I just said is more comprehensible without explanations. To explain is to jam people's thinking.

I am facing elements (Kevin Killian's elements) and finding out that his elements clear the mind. I wish to keep that in mind the longest possible. I'm swimming in a zone where cold water would meet a hot stream, and not mix. I would have preferred to burn entirely rather than...

Today is another day. The speed at which the universe is moving is illimited, so we don't need to bother, an ultimate battle being impossible from the start. We're in the universe, but don't really know where we are. Everything that is is on a scale of its own.

Life is daily, death is eternal; it means that eternity is useless. We live as if we knew that: we hang on details, keep searching, to keep the illusion alive, the illusion that things matter. But is that a mere illusion? I don't always think so.

I am talking to you because I need you, and to need means to love. Let's see. Am I just establishing inventories? Where am I? That's already an enormous question. I am in the midst of whatever I am thinking of. There are fires in California, they have returned. I am burning. Am one of the trees that's disappearing in the fires. My body black and grey becoming ashes.

And what's left? Things enter existence, then do not last. How am I still around, how are my bones still related to my mind? In this mystery is there any window?

The window is in fact a sliding door facing the Atlantic. Its tides, its waves, its whims. And my own expectations, premonitions, fears and delusions. The tides recede, far away, in the direction of England, where some crucial things are happening. Further North. That chapter is closed. So many things are out of reach.

My preoccupation, now, concerns a requiem that I have to write; it cannot be for planet Earth, as it is slowly dying, but not dead. What's gone is the earthly paradise it once was.

There's a dilation of the senses under the heat. Wind surfing on the shore. The summer is drifting, becoming a cloud, the summer is raining.

There's a relation between an inner light which is mine, and the world's exuberance, for example my need to turn to Heraclitus, periodically. There's an equilibrium we all possess, while it eludes us, and the possibility, regardless, of swimming twice in the same river...but when, and where...

The world's energy showed itself in this particular day through the tides: the longest tide in years, it was said, and I watched it, before it disappeared. Sitting at the edge of the unique, long street of Dahouet, closest to the ocean, I looked and looked at the narrow strait where the mounting waters formed a river having the deep and shining green color of pine, hurrying upstream, carrying my senses with it. It's worth giving one's life for a moment like this.

This is a planetary country. We're in a geography that's asking a a question: why is your life so monotonous? The question makes that life bearable.

I need the physical world, that's my sanity. And it's more than that: anything not tied to the physical world sounds suspicious, that's why I rather kick stones with my foot than linger on the world's issues: if none of them have any solution, then why bother? For a prisoner the most important thing is to see the light outside. As for the rest, he'll wait. Nowadays I'm in a similar situation; I yearn for long shadows and the games they play on a wall, for a short trail, for a beach with nobody on it…for the nonsense of a screwball kid.

Now it's time to open the cave's window and leave it open. Let reality fill the space. At what speed? Who cares? The marriage of heaven and hell, a book, or a fact? A good storm will erase all this, and erase the rainbow. At last, we will breathe innocently.

I didn't dream last night, nor the night before, I didn't even sleep. I contemplated the night's different shades, its infinite richness. Once in a while, there were sounds, the night's own music, dispersed. There was some visibility but no particular object came to the fore. I could sense waves, I could see obscurity's own kind of brilliance. There was also thickness to the air. Soft currents traversed that air, barely flowing on my hands. I also sensed that my own body seemed to float more than the rest. Beginnings of visions, more than of ideas, started to cross my mind.

All the shades of blackness, more than the color black, took care of the space. The night went on, repeating itself.

Events. More events. Unexpected ones. A friend's collapse. To witness a mind go wild, like the California fires right now, is the hardest thing one can experience. And still, we do. The mind gets so fluid that you can't stop it with your will, you watch the will's annihilation. The question arises: are we just a series of chemical reactions? If we were courageous enough we would say yes, we are. But there is something in those chemical reactions that make us reject the acknowledgment of their own nature. We're body and soul, we say, let's accept this myth. Plato did it.

Where's the friend? At last, in a clinic. But there's no relief to that churning stomach, to that feeling of insecurity that pervades the very air we breathe, and it's not the time to read the newspaper: they seem to revel in news of accidents, murders, disasters. I have to remind myself that there are still people who lead decent lives, but no consolation seems possible as a circle of metal imprisons my heart.

As a child, I used to dread the time between 4 and 6 in the afternoon. Nothing changed. Four o'clock remains a fatidic hour, four in the afternoon, four close to early morning, the poles of my private time.

It's gray outside, stormy. I am looking at the ocean, it's some ten yards away, I wonder why its tide stops at a certain point, why it doesn't enter my apartment, but I have to live my limitations, so I think that the ocean too has its own destiny.

There's a pale yellowish band above the horizon. Why does a horizon exist? To lift my spirit? Why does a volcano surge in my memory, an old volcano whose slopes have been taken over by plantations of banana trees? It links me to a small garden in Beirut where 2 or 3 trees were short and the bananas heavy. At this very moment that memory is painful, my arm vainly wanting to reach them. They leap across the years. If you wait enough, you may go back to that garden in one of your lives.

Mountains and thunderous rivers belong to a few cells in my brain, or to some corner of paradise. Tonight, for the first time in my own experience of this harbor in Brittany, a large band of fog from west to east underlines the horizon...I must have been homesick for fog, and it arrived!

I lately learned a lot about the tides. The ocean is not just advancing and receding; it's responding to rhythms within its rhythms, frequencies, symmetries, accelerations...it's an organism with a complex and regulated system of breathing, with ways of life dwarfing those that govern us. The ocean is used, and misused, while it's utterly unknown.

Thinking of all that, I fell on a program concerning the planet Mars and projects envisioned for it by a European space agency. The pictures of Mars's surface brought me back to our oceans, but the film was made with a brown coloration that created the feeling that we were facing deserts. A special strangeness pertains to that planet. I have seen in Bloomington, Indiana, some twenty years ago, under a special microscope, a little piece of soil brought back from Mars, and I saw irisations foreign to anything I had seen on Earth. And the same is true for the rock formations and soil configurations that cover that planet. When we land there, we'll be utterly disoriented. We're in dire need of that.

It's dark in here. There are a few distant lights, making us aware that we're living by night. In silence.

In silence, in the dark, the tides shine, get slippery, their fluidity turns them into a mirage. There's a persistent hum to the ocean that translates into a back-and-forth movement of our body. Walls disappear and new visual formations invade the imagination. One is not in usual dimensions. Sleep belongs to the past, and the hours too. Luminosity enmeshed with darkness makes us cross over new territories. You move into galaxies in a few seconds, space-time becomes just a game.

Thinking is dimmed when familiar forms of reality disappear. This is not a loss. Long periods of inner silence favor clearings, they let the light in, the flooding, the blinding, the bedazzlement. We need spaces for the reshuffling of new cards, need to be nowhere. Thinking doesn't always come from preceding thoughts: I suspect it's always being born, even when it seems related to the past.

Tomorrow I'll move out of here, which means I will live with no horizon in sight, I will not lead my days according to the tides, the sky will not enter my room, and my headaches will return. Then, why am I leaving?

Have we lost our autonomy, from conditioning to conditioning, have we become prisoners of webs, cobwebs, tightening circles that make us respond in predictable ways to the situations we face? Is becoming a robot our own end?

I took a train and went through immense plains of a golden hue. The land looked soft, marked here and there by rows of trees. The TGV was roaring. Reluctantly, I reached a city I didn't care for. Have no heart for such a place. But where's my place? Still looking for one, it seems. But I loved so many of them, so deeply. Delphi comes to mind, Mount Tamalpaïs, for sure. And what about Beirut, and Damascus? I should come back on my statement; am looking for almost nothing. Too much of a past, too little ahead, but wait a minute, we always lived day to day, so where's the difference?

There's a loneliness to any ending, but we have felt even lonelier. We climbed peaks to get away from strange pains in the stomach, but we ran into other pains. The light is fading the way it did when we had to return from school, oh the despair children know and hide! I was afraid of the day's end, now I fear the day itself. There were in-between years, but who I was has disappeared since.

We're left on the road, so to speak. It's dark, like the coffee I drank at noon, which prevents me from sleeping so many hours later. I love the night, said it so many times that I consider that a failure, that repetition, but loving anything keeps us going. There are no newspapers tomorrow, so history will wait. Anyway, since Herodotus there have been no reliable historians, unless you think that some writers, such as Tolstoy, have been. I will agree with you on that. But Tolstoy is not writing in the *New York Times* anymore.

Then why am I writing these lines which are not bringing much to the world? It's one of those things that people do, that's all. There's in each of us the hidden belief that somehow we matter, the way we say Black Lives Matter. It's true.

I picked up a ribbon that had fallen from a package, and something told me that I had Ariadne's thread in my hand...and I'm finding myself on the way to the Minotaur, scared to death, but called as by a magnet. The fear itself has a mesmerizing power. The labyrinth is in Crete, where it used to be. There have been landslides around but the sacred pattern has held.

I would have been an archeologist, and would have found a necklace in pure gold, and wondered to whom it had belonged. Not necessarily a woman. I'm a passenger on planet Earth, itself a passerby. The empire crushed as if it were made of cardboard, and we retrieved some memories which will die with us, or survive, for a while... But everything lasts just for a while, probably eternity itself.

What can one do about melancholic moods? I wonder. I don't know. They kept me company for so long that they even aged with me. They took me to airports and railway stations. I would have missed them, had they disappeared, yes, I would have; our friends are not necessarily human. (Too human?)

The early hours of the day are more mysterious than the evenings: there's freshness to them, the paleness of youth. You wouldn't mind if night returned, but it doesn't. You will have to put up with the chaos you know too well, and suddenly, sometimes, you will recover the pre-dawns that preceded your early-morning dreams.

Speaking of dreams: I crossed the Golden Gate Bridge on my way to Mount Shasta. The fog moved in and I waited until it was followed by swarms of pelicans and I waited again, confusing hours with seconds, and Shasta appeared closer, covered totally with snow, and I turned my back, finding

myself sailing on an ocean filled with sharks. The
world is crowded.

Narration is an outdated form. It's prehistoric.
This exercise in futility is close to dying, though
it may go on for years. This smoke-screen for
anguish takes us nowhere, save to misguided pub-
lishers. So we flip-flop toward that core of reality
we call silence by talking and writing, illustrat-
ing the degree of incoherence our humanity has
reached. There's something hypnotic to aligning
words, something addictive. That's probably all
there is to writing.

The universe makes a sound—is a sound. In the
core of this sound there's a silence, a silence that
creates that sound, which is not its opposite, but its
inseparable soul. And this silence can also be heard.

This silence is the preparation of things to come,
but is not free standing. It's rather the shadow
of whatever is, which precedes or follows at will

any element that presents itself to this world. Its favorite time is the night. In my view, California nights, streaked with the lights of trucks crisscrossing the land.

My favorite time is in time's other side, its other identity, the kind that collapses and sometimes reappears, and sometimes doesn't. The one that looks like marshmallows, pomegranates, and stranger things, before returning to its kind of abstraction. I used to be fond of time as it was a matter that helped us feel intelligent. Those days have gone to where days go, in their own cemeteries. Today I see eternity everywhere. I had yesterday an empty glass of champagne on the table, and it looked both infinite and eternal, though it left me indifferent. At least, I was in good company, and a day closer to all sorts of annihilations.

The French added two major statements to the world's cultures: "Je pense, donc je suis," and "Je est un autre." We may disagree by stating "I don't think, but I am" which can equally make sense. And it's also possible to think that "the I refuses to be shared by an other I." Who would dare say that it shouldn't?

In every place I live there are bookshelves and filled with books I never read, and that, mathematically, I will not have the time to read. I contemplate them. They're so aloof, so silent. I spend hours next to them. When in Brittany hearing the ocean, there's a photograph of Tolstoy on one of the shelves, Tolstoy old and thin, in a housecoat with which he used to go out of the house, looking exactly like my father who in his last days had already become his own ghost, and was terrifying me, mostly at night, in the quietness of the whole neighborhood.

Today Nick Hoff landed in Paris. Have not seen him yet, have not for years, remembering some nights at Specs, on San Francisco's Columbus Avenue. I read *Some Ones*, his latest book, which is what the breeze will bring to you when it has barely touched some elements around... North Beach has heard Miles Davis and Jack Spicer with their different instruments: the human voice, the trumpet. It still listens to poets, it does. You have to meet them. My days are both too long and too short for letting me know what I want to do. So I watch them go by...Heraclitus standing there.

I am not in a hurry to live, am not in a hurry to die; I am just talking to you. You could be coming back from Delphi, where I would have liked to be, there, under a stormy sky, with clouds trembling, with the columns hiding in fog, with the past intact, with the Phoenician gifts unpacked, with everything waiting. I am in Delphi; how would I know I'm not?

Actioned by a fever, as usual, always projected, this engine we call life, or existence, that we carry in us and still search for, always at a loss, running, and running, and not moving ahead, like planet Earth blindly turning in circles, until we both disappear from the screen. I have no strategy, for anything, in fact. Will not boil an egg, will rather go down to the restaurant that just opened next door. You sit, you eat, you go back home; you call that a day. Who will put up with despair? Some desperate humans, for sure.

One of them was Rainer Maria Rilke who wrote his journal under the guise of Malte Laurids Brigge! That's the south of Central Europe for you. Joyce sitting in the theatre in Trieste. Poets losing the North Star.

There's something I can do that fills me with happiness: get up in the middle of the night and watch the sky, the nights covered with stars. This doesn't happen in cities anymore, but lately, in Brittany, it happened, and quite often, and the sight is mesmerising. You would think that you're back to the nights of the gods, the Chinese ones, the Babylonian ones, the Greek ones, the prehistoric ones that we ignore and who must have been awesome, and must have been playing their kind of football with all these celestial creatures. In those nights windows are in the way.

There's, under it all, a tremendous weakness that's eating at our souls: it's true that I saw "in one night, all nights," and that recently in Berlin my statement was written on the wall of a church bombed in '45, and partially standing, sheltering indifferently the heat or the snow. But I'm trembling. I will disappear before having found a convincing answer to this question: what's the Absolute? At the end we ended up deciding that the Absolute is a misnomer. We fell into facts, such as the fact of being hungry, the fact that the atom bomb is being constantly improved...to put it simply, we're suffocating.

That's why we find in some events some moments of lightness: I speak of the dinner last night at home with Nick Hoff, and Sciascia, a simple dinner in a simply friendly atmosphère, moments stolen, mysterious, given the weight of the air that we're breathing.

Then, again, this sentiment that nothing is happening returned! The world is thick with events, and I dare say, it's empty. That's our predicament. I don't believe that it's empty only in rare moments. Watching the tides gets me close to the absolute, an absolute which is in movement, and watery. The feeling that each moment repeats the one that presided over the creation of the world overwhelms me with bliss. But then, I also don't believe in creation, but rather in the universe's eternity, which then will imply its immobility, and that thought fills me with sacred terror. Things go that way.

We also think in ways we're not aware of. That sounds like a paradox, or nonsense, but I'm serious. I experienced double thinking: one thought sliding on another, was startled, didn't know which one to follow, lost sight of both. I was also slightly scared: are thoughts bouncing balls? Do we really own them?

The trees are yellowing, giving the air a metallic tone, shaking the imagination out of its lethargy. The outside world brings much more to me than what we call the inner one. Yes there's all the horror we know, but Cash Creek in Yolo County, the upper Hudson, the Nile under its pharaonic hues, Mount Shasta under the rain, and the mountain, the one which is mine, take me into their own identities, they silence the world.

I want to go rafting, not only on rivers but on any experience, the mental ones particularly, feel the joy of frantic concepts, of their freedom mainly. It's tiring to analyze, cut thinking into bits, scrutinize happenings, so much labor for mediocre results. Let's jump and dive, go with winds, let's get wet and even hurt, let's give the Yellowstone River the

chance to toss us the way it does tree trunks and
salmon, let's use its ways on our dormant brains!

Where do painters stand in all this? Usually,
nowhere. They seldom say, or write something as
revelatory as their works can be, structurally non-
translatable. I miss listening to jazz music, or to
Schubert, and if I had the chance, would rather
watch a tiger run for real than read my most
beloved poets. But poets are poets. Nothing will
dislodge them. Even when in their most pathetic
moments, they're badly needed.

Somebody is going to Moscow, a friend. It's colder
over there, their winters being always in a hurry.
We must reread Malevitch, the only theologian
that communism has produced. Don't try to make
sense of what he says, look at his works, they will
inscribe themselves on the cells of your body.

I will paint a red square to make an echo of the
black one that accompanied him during his

funerals. Looking back at Malevitch is inhabiting the future. His fierce spirituality works like a rocket: angels must shake their wings, dust off their halos, we can do the same, cast off our traditional beliefs, discover new territories that lay between abstraction and the journeys of the senses. Why don't we dare go behind the horizon line?

The telephone rang: my friend Claire Paget called me to tell that she was watching from her sliding glass wall a patch of white cloud that returns regularly, in the same shape and at the same hour. "That little cloud comes every afternoon," she said, "it's funny, I have ended up relating to it, talking to it, you know what I mean, it's up there, now I'm waiting for it, and it's coming." That's the type of thing I would dream for myself.

But clouds have a way to elude us, to leave us sitting like duds, to wave us goodbye. Today was the day when I faced their absence's importance, when a shattering experience occured: my friend

Matthieu Cénac brought me casually a book he has just published, *1 the Road* by writer Ross Goodwin. The book is described on the cover as "The first gonzo Artificial Neural Network is a genius writer."

I opened the book and started reading the stanzas written with artificial intelligence and started shaking, and the destabilization lasted for quite a while. My stomach has been churning, an avalanche of questions going in all directions overwhelmed my mind: the poems written are beautiful; that's what's maddening. I will transcribe a few ones:

It was nine seventeen in the morning, and the house was heavy.

It was seven minutes to ten o'clock in the morning, and it was the only good thing that had happened.

What is it? The painter asked.

And we ask: what is poetry? An urgency has here been created, a challenge to the answers we had, an upheaval in metaphysics...I thought: from now on, anything will do; it's not the poet who's the poet, it's only the reader!

And what about intelligence? As the difference between things is narrowing, and in all fields, such as, for example, the traditional gap between the genders that is narrowing, intelligence as we knew it, and artificial intelligence, are all due to come closer and closer...in this experiment in poetry they have probably merged, tempting us to think that nothing is ultimately artificial; that Reality has to always be real.

In the noise that in some spaces becomes a clamor how would I ever find a way out? The process started at birth, for you, for me. Miles of walks in different cities, as if from nowhere to nowhere some peace will be found. Was it found? It's maybe facing me. A piece of bread, a serving of cheese in quietness, is that what will lead us to the divine? Why shouldn't it?!

Bread and cheese...Psomi ke feta...the café Adonis in Sopelos with its chairs painted in blue, its tables too, and straight ahead the blue sea under the blue sky and the whiteness of the cheese and the somnolence in the head, that's my paradise...the incense smelling Greek churches... my own kind of the great promise.

To use the nobility of language for all the trash we hear is such a punishment. I'm in search of a special state of silence, not the one when you can hear the circulation of your blood in your veins, not the one that's heard when the music is over, not the one...a silence between eons of silence.

Would you follow a bankrupt banker? To start, I have to find one. I do not work for the government, so the question leaves me indifferent. But things go deeper: I'm not unhappy enough to follow anything or anybody, as desires don't call me often.

My dreams are short: they're imitating the new wave of videos. Even in dreams we lose concentration. To prove to myself that I'm not quite dead, I reread Barrett Watten's "Plan B." In all innocence he can call that piece of thinking a manifesto. A manifesto as stirring as the *Manifeste du Surréalisme* had been when it appeared in 1924. These texts are territories: you can walk in them, you can drive, or fly over. "Plan B," among other things, already challenges artificial intelligence. It beats it, because I doubt that artificial intelligence will concern itself with man's destiny.

We have to deal with hopelessness. We hoped, and hoped, and ended up with the the atomic bomb and the death of God. We are here, stranded in an airport, queuing for some extraterrestrial destination, for just displacing our fears.

It's Paris now, under fog. The Eiffel Tower is turned into a smudge, a faint mark on pure space. People's hands are in their pockets, the river Seine feels icy. You have to walk fast to keep some warmth in you. All the international tractations sound ridiculous compared to the simple, basic questions that we ask: do angels still care? Is the human species going to survive, and, by the way, is this very question really important? Is God really dead, and if He is, what good did that death ever bring? Has love become obsolete, would it be endangered by artificial intelligence?

Fog brings me closer to what I call my soul. There's an affinity between those darkening mists and my state of mind, a movement from the one to the other, both ways, probably even an exchange of substance...a mystery I can approach, I can hear, although it's made mainly of silence.

Fog is the resolution of divinity; the domain of the Greek gods, their residency, as they haven't died. I hear the fog as if it were the swish of the leaves of a forest. I see it swell. As it is possessed, I see it slide over the land as a divine warrior. Sometimes I wonder if I won't end my life in a kind of a fusion with one of its curves.

Imagination arrives from the cosmos's farthest reaches and elects our brain the way it would a harbor, establishes its headquarters, and soon starts its misdoings. But what would we have done without it? Hell would have been tidier.

California's beauty is so intense that it raises our temperature. I spent many nights in Yosemite Valley, with wings behind my arms, ready to take off. California was then made of luminous rays, of sounds, of yearnings. It wasn't necessary to think of boundaries, of the atmosphere...outer space used to start at the cabin, or next door.

Like Icarus, I fell. I fell on the valley's floor. Close to a waterfall. Then I rolled over some highways, covered miles, reached sea level, the Pacific. That had its own magic. For reasons of no interest per se, I ended in Paris...an end, indeed. There are comfortable corners in hell, very few are those who know that, but I do.

There are places that seem to be where they ought to be, but they are in some parallel world and I reside in one of them.

While you're young, you die many times. It's an adventure into which you run head-on, it's the great discovery of loss. Then, years go by, or pile up, they carry you on their waters, and show you that next time death will be for keeps, that the space I just mentioned has a single door opening on the Void, and you realize that reality used to come only in bits, to each his/her allotted package, to each his/her particular length of rope.

But there are still great escapes, mythical ones. There are, indeed, mythical experiments, like the one that happened just today, the landing (the Marsing?) of the latest spacecraft sent from Earth, and its explorer meant to probe the innards of the planet Mars.

We're in prehistory, the heroic age of the space age, we're the cavemen of the capsules that embark for the universe.

I have followed the space experiments since Gagarin's historic attempt at breaking the wall of gravity. It was the most exhilarating event of the times. We were in the fateful year of 1958. We had escaped the power of Earth. Ever since, we've been floating in the universe, attracted by its boundlessness. We will have to chase away whatever has occupied our mind up to now in order to contemplate these new territories (and solitudes) that we will face.

The solitudes will be new experiences, their newness may bring defiance to our curiosity, may shake off the weariness we will for sure carry as a shadow. I am facing right now a Martian land-scape, and by establishing a mental interplanetary link, I become an extraterrestrial being, and, O miracle, I'm fully happy!

Back to Earth, tonight, this very night, I am abso-lutely absorbed by the memory, the persistent image of Lydia Yourtchenko, a face, and a name, that has accompanied me for years and years, since I was about eighteen. Tonight, I will take time off, and keep her in this house. Planets and galaxies will not distract me. Nothing will.

We will always be somewhere, and at some point, enmeshed in cosmic forces, tributary to ancestry, involved in social circles, finger printed, filed and identified, meaning never free, but then would death when it comes mean freedom? That radical experience will be no experience, as it won't be shared, and evaluated, and discussed, no, it will be a radical passage, a passing, a spilling over, death as the end of language, the end of being at the heart of Being.

I brought my friend back but in fact what did I do, as she remained invisible? I am not given to being satisfied by half-measure, so I remained with an intact need to see her. Yes, she is gone for decades by now, as if snatched away. I'm thinking: how happy those who believe in resurrection must be. I believe too, sometimes, but in moral resurrection. And in something more which has nothing to do with the return of the dead. It's a form of myopia, maybe, but I am helpless on that matter. I see sometimes an openness and I hurry into it. I understand the need for an absolute, but the absolute never has become an entity, an object, even spiritual, or God. I reached the absolute, in rare moments, but as a form of radical thinking, thinking pushed to its end, to its silencing, to something like the revelation of itself.

An absence is a form of silence. Is the space from which language has vanished. The disappearance of answers. But it's not necessarily a void. Where is Lydia? Orpheus wondered: where's Euridyce, where? He thought that he found out she was nowhere. But in this moment Lydia has a form of existence which is not ordinary existence, as she is forever invisible. Then, is my search a way of trying to bring her resurrection?

The silence that surrounds me makes her absence most acute but at the same time gives her a strange kind of presence: I get to be caught within meta-physical mirrors. I am confused, or, rather, I am realizing that being, or not being, cannot be dealt with with thinking, but are matters of experience, experienced often in murky waters, and that their intensity creates waves that invade us, that leave us stunned. There's no resolution to somebody's final absence.

I took the train for Erquy in my desire to avoid the holidays. One more year is ending, a leaf is taken away from the book that's supposed to be one's life. I am back where I belong, facing an ocean. The horizon is clear. There are road repairs down the street, much noise, a lot of dust. But the ocean is doing its favorite activity: up, and down, and up again...the tides

This very small town is quiet. The stores, with a few exceptions, are closed. No junk to celebrate what used to be the birth of a baby God. No. Just a few places to get something to eat. This town is not linked to my past, to any portion of it, it's therefore restful. I should say it's friendly. It looks transient, like all small harbors. The seagulls are gone, which makes the sky even more peaceful, the kind of peace that survives tempests.

I don't hear many things, as my hearing is poor, and welcome this form of rest. I need nights to spill on my days, want to roam through forests, run into abandoned castles, I want to see rivers hidden in unexpected valleys. I want the sun to be soft.

We're at the door of Time's immensity. And some of us want to kill, as if we're even worthy of being killed. And why do we put some killers, though the weaker ones, in jail? We should have long conversations with them, reach some of the depths of human nature. We must listen to some of these tales, to the cries of despair, to the darkness of their experiences. This is what Dostoyevsky has done. Already an epileptic, already terrified, he went to encounters with terror, because the abyss has dimensions, because mysteries inhabit bottomless pits. In the meantime, what we call our life is spent always in expectation.

The day is blustery, one more day following an infinity of days. And this one on its way out, according to its fate. If everything is alive, this day is too, a life independent from mine, and still interdependant. And the ocean is itself life's immensity. Its salt is in the air, burning my skin. Salt in my eyes. The sky is black, before nighttime. Strange things happen in winter, in this silence. A few sailors take to the high seas. Gusts of wind shake the waters, bend the tree trunks. Everything turns in circles.

The wind returns. It carries voices. Armies surge from behind the clouds and invade the beaches. This is not the proper way to celebrate the end of the season, of the year. Not many days are left before the feast of the Nativity, and we have these armies running on the seashore, escalating the walls. There's nobody around, people went inland. I'm alone in the apartment, watching. I will not move.

The armies spread. They're out to cover the whole coast, they're having fun. It must be useless to be scared, but the people are gone. Then, I mean now, the rain has started to fall. It's becoming a storm. A tempest. The soldiers will get wet, some will catch a cold. A radio station is still working, it says that hordes of soldiers have been dying, in fact, melting away.

But again, a day has gone by. It went on foot, on a horse, or in some ways that we're not equipped to know, and what am I left with? I know what's left in me, under these clouds, this wind, this cold, this wintry weather: the need to be in Greece. Will I die without returning to Delphi, to Athens? (to Beirut, to the Headlands, by the Pacific?!). I remember Maria Farandouri in the lobby of the hotel which sits at the foot of the Acropolis, I remember her singing Theodorakis. And the Mediterranean has colors that the Atlantic, at least around here, hasn't even imagined. Are older people on death row? Don't tell them that.

Delphi still waits for the offerings of the tribes. Nothing is coming, it seems. The oracle got discouraged, tired of predicting our disasters, our guiltless presidents and dictators. She got tired of watching the joy, the bliss felt by the "rulers" of our world when they unleash their total wars. She's silent. There's no past, there's no future, so she went into deep sleep. If you're interested, you can go and hear her sleep, if you dare.

Back to days. This one has been exceptional: I haven't seen a single human being, a single living thing. The breeze did not stir. The telephone didn't ring. I did not go out, went on the deck, saw nobody. I slept late this morning, and will go to bed pretty soon. A perfect day for banana fish.

France is in ebullition. It doesn't want a revolution, it wants more money. A bitter taste in the mouth, water stops running through a faucet, the end of utopias. We're always a generation behind reality. Do you want to quit this world on such a sour note? Isn't quitting always tinged with some form of melancholy, or is melancholy itself out of fashion, who's going to tell?

It's always late at night that the most persistent questions arise. I feel deprived of the things that used to carry me forward, forward to this day. No,

I am not impressed by achievements, I am rather sinking under all kinds of worries...I see Earth as barren as Mars, as inhospitable. I just saw a picture of a frozen lake on Mars whose diameter is supposed to be 50 kilometers. It's a pinkish land covered with ice. It can catch one's attention, but it reminds me that we see other planets in terms of our own. If we're going to carry this Earth on our backs wherever we go—which seems to be the case—why should we bother to travel to such distant places? It will look like divorcing to just remarry the same kind of person. I shouldn't be talking, as I always felt marriage to be a most claustrophobic situation. We never have enough breathing space. To breathe, what a luxury!

France never interested me per se, but it happens that I can't fly out, and there's more to it, a life-long personal history interwoven with this country's own history. I will disappear without having solved the turbulent emotions that seize me when I think of her: its whole colonial past and the remnants of that past that are stuck in my throat. It's a dark stone in a long tunnel, a residency in a labyrinth which has no way out.

I spent Christmas Eve in the restaurant next door, where there was some festive mood, subdued, pleasant. Today was one of those non-days, as if in a parenthesis, but I had the pleasure of seeing one of Simone's new sculptures: a "Trojan Horse," the one that wrote Greek History with a torch.

We have ways to distract ourselves from our destinies. I don't know how, we just play it by instinct. We manage to take our attention away, into outer space, into a history book, into our own imaginations, or just a post-card, but we do, we go.

For today, I went shamelessly into food, ate panettone, and rice-pudding done the oriental way, listened to the news announcing a shutdown of the federal government, and wondered if whole nations drift the way an individual will, drift aimlessly, almost blissfully, like on a ski slope nobody had foreseen. Oh everything is eventually overcome.

China landed on the hidden side of the Moon! We have seen the first pictures taken by a space probe on the dark side of the campanion of Earth, a breakthrough for the new year, a crack on the wall, an opening! I felt the grounds open up under my feet, I felt I reached a landmark of cosmic proportion. I drank beer differently than usual.

Then I read about Sargon of Akkad's construction of the first empire in the Land of the Two Rivers. It made me think of the reality that we will face pretty soon: A dreadful sameness is invading our world, which is becoming a megalopolis, an extension of Las Vegas and Dubai. To escape that suffocation we will go to outer space, and we will go back into Time, to the past through archeology, back to Babylon or the cities buried under the Amazon river...the sameness that's taking hold of our present is propulsing us into these extremes that we'll call the New Age. My hands are getting cold, a musician is playing Bach on a lute on television, and it fits: Bach's music is the needle of the cosmic balance.

This has taken me into the core of a silence that underlines the universe: underneath the mesh of sounds that never cease there's a strange phenomena, a counter-reality, the rolling of silent matter.

Silence is a flower, it opens up, dilates, extends its texture, can grow, mutate, return on its steps. It can watch other flowers grow and become what they are. We're at the turn of the year, I have to invite somebody or something. The live thickness of the silence makes sounds free themselves and expand. The year is turning, has turned, 2018 is gone forever, gone into being the new year, people are dancing, 2019 has just entered, wide-eyed, utterly new.

Silence is the creation of space, a space that memory needs to use…an incubator. We're dealing here with dimensions, stretching inner muscles, pushing aside any interference. We're dealing with numbers, but not counting. Silence demands the nature of night, even in full day, it demands shadows.

But in all my wanderings I never forgot the light: the skies in the Orient I know, the particular one that covers Lebanon, Syria, Egypt…the ones of the Eastern Mediterranean which is neither Provence, nor Spain, are dripping light over silent villages, for hours and in between hours, turning the air into luminescence, creating the mystery of hues, as the sun itself melts in waters.

I consider the light that enters the room in the early hours of the day as a messenger of the sun, a direct voyager, a particle, a wave, who knows, but an object of sorts that left its solar source, covered miles, and landed on my skin. So the universe constantly visits us while waiting for us to reverse that itinerary.

Then I receive in an email the picture of a cabin near Joshua Tree, and of a dog. An affinity between the two. The scene speaks of the light over there, bathing the desert, and of the form that destiny is taking today.

Speaking of destiny, how to say why the moon has been so present throughout my life, why she traversed the sky so often, so insistently, sometimes even in daytime, how did it happen that she practically took center stage? And now, at last, the Chinese probe Chang'e 4 lands on her hidden side, and we see craters relatively close to each other, and in their astonishment of facing an instrument that came from Earth, they seem to be more silent than ever. That curved surface is suffused with being, with the fact of being there, with the need to return to its autonomy. I myself have been there but did not disturb. My eyes are no instruments. They moved over that area with the power of the imagination, a power borrowed, but more trustworthy than anything else.

So I have had since childhood those long though instantaneous voyages to the most visible of all the planets. I felt sometimes frozen and sometimes too warm, but I went, and acquired a magic sense of isolation.

There were years when I wanted to read by moonlight, drive by it...My eyes got strained, policemen stopped me on the roads, but I tried time and time again. I also wondered: are the moon's radiations more dangerous than the sun's? Why do we speak of lunacy? What was Shakespeare's relationship to the moon?

I have invited to my banquet you and your neighbor, and animals too, and stones and mountains, rivers will bring their floods. I will tell you history is made of wars, of ideas, of misery, of glory preceding misery. History is made of everything that has ever happened, the whole trajectory of humans, of dirt and galaxies. You are History, the squirrel is History, the Universe is History. It includes God too.

Since, some very strange things did happen. I have been visited for a few days by lines and lines of ghost-like creatures. They came in various dimensions, various sizes, and colors. Children were running, and one morning they had book-bags, dressed warmly, and looked late for school. Most everybody was stylized, drawn flat rather than three-dimentional. Some were disquietingly tall, were reaching the ceiling with their heads, and coming dangerously close to my neck.

I also fell ill. A new virus, it seems, killed some 6000 people all over France. It didn't finish me off, but came close. New pains were experienced, unwelcome. It lasted four good months. I still feel shaky, unsure.

I am a barren planet. Empty spaces, with no vegetation, but with the illusion that I smell thyme. When I reach an edge I see other planets, non-hospitable ones. Then I return to my module, my isolation: I think of the ocean, the steel-colored surface of the Pacific, and of my mountain, and try not to cry.

Silent and undeclared loves become unwinged angels, subject to gravity, just like us. They were made by Simone for her latest show in Marrakech, in the forms of a scarab, probably an instinctive return to the sacred beetle referring to the ancient Egyptian god of the sun. Recently, I had to invent a new angelic order of astronaut-angels, trumpeting their existence.

I needed them to accompany those of the human race who are on their way to settle in outer space. They will appear in a requiem to be performed at the next Venice Biennial.

Writing that requiem I had to hear the representative of those humans who claim that they are tired of the world's situation and that they will be looking for a new Revelation. But the choir kept telling them that Revelation is indivisible. It's one. It's very likely what was meant by Nietzsche when he mentioned, "the eternal return of the same."

Night functions like the snow. Erases the landscape.

Etel Adnan was born in Beirut, Lebanon in 1925. She studied philosophy at the Sorbonne, U.C. Berkeley, and at Harvard, and taught at Dominican College in San Rafael, California, from 1958–1972. In solidarity with the Algerian War of Independence (1954–1962), Adnan began to resist the political implications of writing in French and became a painter. Then, through her participation in the movement against the Vietnam War (1959–1975), she began to write poetry and became, in her words, "an American poet." In 1972, she returned to Beirut and worked as cultural editor for two daily newspapers— first for *Al Safa*, then for *L'Orient le Jour*. Her novel *Sitt Marie-Rose*, published in Paris in 1977, won the France-Pays Arabes award and has been translated into more than ten languages. In 1977, Adnan re-established herself in California, making Sausalito her home, with frequent stays in Paris. Adnan is the author of more than a dozen books in English, including *Journey to Mount Tamalpais* (1986); *The Arab Apocalypse* (1989); *In the Heart of the Heart of Another Country* (2005); *Sea and Fog* (2012), winner of the Lambda Literary Award for Lesbian Poetry and the California Book Award for Poetry, *Night* (2016), and *Surge* (2018). *Time*, a volume of her poems translated from French into English by Sarah Riggs, received the 2020 International Griffin Poetry Prize. In 2014, she was awarded one of France's highest cultural honors: l'Ordre de Chevalier des Arts et Lettres. Adnan's paintings have been widely exhibited, including Documenta 13, the Whitney Biennial, The New Museum, SFMOMA, and Museum der Moderne Salzburg. Mathaf: Arab Museum of Modern and the Serpentine Galleries have mounted retrospectives of her work. She now lives in France.

NIGHTBOAT BOOKS

Nightboat Books, a nonprofit organization, seeks to develop audiences for writers whose work resists convention and transcends boundaries. We publish books rich with poignancy, intelligence, and risk. Please visit nightboat.org to learn about our titles and how you can support our future publications.

The following individuals have supported the publication of this book. We thank them for their generosity and commitment to the mission of Nightboat Books:

Kazim Ali
Anonymous
Jean C. Ballantyne
Photios Giovanis
Amanda Greenberger
Elizabeth Motika
Benjamin Taylor
Peter Waldor
Jerrie Whitfield & Richard Motika

In addition, this book has been made possible, in part, by grants from the New York City Department of Cultural Affairs in partnership with the City Council and the New York State Council on the Arts Literature Program.